MEGHAN MARKLE

Mitchell Lane
PUBLISHERS
2001 SW 31st Avenue
Hallandale, FL 33009
www.mitchelllane.com

Tammy
Gagne

PUBLISHERS

Printing   1   2   3   4   5   6   7   8   9

A Robbie Reader Biography

Aaron Rodgers
Abigail Breslin
Adam Levine
Adrian Peterson
Albert Einstein
Albert Pujols
Aly and AJ
Andrew Luck
AnnaSophia Robb
Ariana Grande
Ashley Tisdale
Brenda Song
Brittany Murphy
Bruno Mars
Buster Posey
Carmelo Anthony
Charles Schulz
Chris Johnson
Clayton Kershaw
Cliff Lee
Colin Kaepernick
Dak Prescott
Dale Earnhardt Jr.
Darius Rucker
David Archuleta
Debby Ryan
Demi Lovato

Derek Carr
Derrick Rose
Donovan McNabb
Drake Bell & Josh Peck
Dr. Seuss
Dustin Pedroia
Dwayne Johnson
Dwyane Wade
Dylan & Cole Sprouse
Ed Sheeran
Emily Osment
Ezekiel Elliott
Hailee Steinfeld
Harry Styles
Hilary Duff
Jamie Lynn Spears
Jennette McCurdy
Jeremy Lin
Jesse McCartney
Jimmie Johnson
Joe Flacco
Johnny Gruelle
Jonas Brothers
Keke Palmer
Kristaps Porzingis
Larry Fitzgerald

LeBron James
Meghan Markle
Mia Hamm
Michael Strahan
Miguel Cabrera
Miley Cyrus
Miranda Cosgrove
Philo Farnsworth
Prince Harry
Raven-Symoné
Rixton
Robert Griffin III
Roy Halladay
Shaquille O'Neal
Story of Harley-Davidson
Sue Bird
Syd Hoff
Tiki Barber
Tim Howard
Tim Lincecum
Tom Brady
Tony Hawk
Troy Polamalu
Tyler Perry
Victor Cruz
Victoria Justice

Library of Congress Cataloging-in-Publication Data
[APPLIED FOR]

ABOUT THE AUTHOR: Tammy Gagne is the author of numerous books for adults and children, including *Prince Harry* and *Ed Sheeran* for Mitchell Lane Publishers. She resides in northern New England with her husband and son. One of her favorite pastimes is visiting schools to speak to kids about the writing process..

PUBLISHER'S NOTE: The following story has been thoroughly researched and to the best of our knowledge represents a true story. While every possible effort has been made to ensure accuracy, the publisher will not assume liability for damages caused by inaccuracies in the data, and makes no warranty on the accuracy of the information contained herein. This story has not been authorized or endorsed by Meghan Markle.

CONTENTS

Words in bold type can be found in the glossary.

Meghan visits the Titanic Belfast during her and Prince Harry's visit to Northern Ireland on March 23, 2018, in Belfast, Northern Ireland, United Kingdom.

1 MAKING A DIFFERENCE

Dustin was in the middle of playing his favorite video game when his little sister stumbled past the television. Although it was the middle of July, Sandy was wearing their mother's white winter coat and tan high heels.

"Did you get into Mom's closet again?" Dustin asked while setting the controller down. Sandy was always playing dress-up. It was anyone's guess whose closet she would raid in the process.

"Yes, now guess who I am," she insisted.

"Someone who is going to be in big trouble if Mom catches you wearing those,"

> **Sandy was always playing dress-up.**

CHAPTER 1

Dustin told her in his deepest big-brother voice.

"I'm a princess!" she belted out, ignoring his warning.

"Princesses don't dress like that," he said. "Now let's put Mom's things back." As he led her upstairs, though, Sandy informed him just how wrong he was.

> **Meghan Markle had been donating her time to worthy causes long before she married Prince Harry in 2018.**

"Real princesses don't have to wear frilly dresses," she shared. "They dress classy and do important things—like help people in need. Meghan Markle and Kate Middleton are princesses. I want to be just like them."

"Actually, they aren't princesses," he told her as he slipped the white coat off her shoulders. "They are duchesses."

"That's not what matters," she told him as she stepped out of her mother's shoes. "What matters is that they spend their lives helping others. I want to do that. I saw on the news that they help kids in Uganda by building schools. I could help build a school. Where is Daddy's tool set?"

Dustin tried to hide his giggle. He loved his little sister's enthusiastic spirit. But babysitting her sure was exhausting.

Meghan Markle had been donating her time to worthy causes long before she married Prince Harry in 2018. When they became engaged the year before, however, she decided to join her husband in his **humanitarian** work through the Royal Foundation, which he founded with the Duke and Duchess of Cambridge. Together, the two royal couples are bringing awareness and change to problems around the globe.

Duke and Duchess of Cambridge, Kate Middleton and Prince William

2 DRAWING HER OWN BOX

Rachel Meghan Markle was born on August 4, 1981, in Los Angeles, California. Her parents, Doria Ragland and Thomas Markle, both worked in television when they met in the 1970s. Her father was a lighting director for a soap opera while her mother was working a temp job at the studio. Doria would later become a yoga instructor and a social worker.

Meghan has said that the Los Angeles neighborhood where she grew up wasn't the most **diverse** place. Doria was African-American. But Meghan looked more like her father, who was Caucasian. When Doria went out with her daughter, people frequently

Doria would later become a yoga instructor and a social worker.

Meghan and her mother, Doria Ragland, attend the UN Women's 20th Anniversary of the Fourth World Conference of Women in Beijing at Manhattan Center at Hammerstein Ballroom on March 10, 2015, in New York City.

asked her where the child's mother was. Many people just assumed that Doria was Meghan's nanny.

Meghan's parents worked hard to lessen how different their daughter felt. Meghan remembers wanting a set of dolls when she was about seven. The set came with either all white dolls or all black ones. To make the toys look more like her family, Thomas bought one of each set. He then put together a special set just for her with an African-American mother and a Caucasian father.

> **Meghan's parents worked hard to lessen how different their daughter felt.**

Other people's assumptions continued to pop up as Meghan got older. When she was in middle school, she had to fill out paperwork one day that demanded she choose between being white and being black. Her teacher told her to check the box for white because of how she looked. But she wasn't just one or the other. When Meghan told her father how torn this made her feel, he told her that if this sort of thing happened again to draw her own box. That advice stayed with her because it made her realize that she shouldn't let other people define her.

3 FINDING THE RIGHT ROLE

Meghan attended an all-girls Catholic school in Los Angeles. When her parents divorced in 1987, Meghan kept living with her mother. But she spent time with her father regularly. By this time he was working on the set of the TV show *Married . . . with Children*. She would hang out on the set with him every day after school. She eventually became inspired to pursue a career in acting.

After graduating from high school, Meghan enrolled in Northwestern University's School of Communication, in Evanston, Illinois. There, she studied theater and international relations before graduating in

When her parents divorced in 1987, Meghan kept living with her mother.

2003. Even before she was done with school, though, she was already performing small parts in such shows as *General Hospital, CSI: NY*, and *90210*. She also appeared in films such as *Get Him to the Greek* and *Horrible Bosses*.

Although she was working here and there, she wasn't getting any big roles. In a piece she wrote for *Elle* magazine, Meghan recalled, "I wasn't black enough for the black roles and I wasn't white enough for the white ones, leaving me somewhere in

Meghan at ELLE's 2nd Annual Women In Television Celebratory Dinner in January 2013

the middle as the ethnic **chameleon** who couldn't book a job."

While she was still struggling to make a living as an actress, she relied on her beautiful handwriting abilities to support herself. Many actresses take jobs as waitresses while they try out for parts. But Meghan worked as a **calligrapher**, creating beautiful invitations and other fancy cards for companies such as Dolce & Gabbana. She has said that the secret to this art form is patience. It cannot be rushed.

> Before finding regular work as an actress, Meghan appeared on the television game show *Deal or No Deal.*

Before finding regular work as an actress, Meghan appeared on the television game show *Deal or No Deal.* She was one of the models who held numbered briefcases—one of which contained the $1 million prize. She said this was definitely a job she did to make

Meghan opens a briefcase containing $500,000 on Episode 228 of Deal or No Deal.

ends meet. But she credits it with teaching her how much she wanted to be doing something else.

4 BIG CHANGES

Meghan's big break finally came in 2011 when she was hired by the USA Network show *Suits*. Meghan has called Rachel Zane her "Goldilocks" job—it was the first role for which she was just right. Rachel was a smart, confident, and beautiful **paralegal** working in a New York law firm. The show quickly became a big success.

Shortly after college, Meghan had begun dating film producer Trevor Engelson. The couple dated six years before becoming engaged in 2010. They married a year later in Jamaica. But their work kept them apart much of the time. While Meghan worked on the *Suits* set in Toronto, Engelson worked

Shortly after college, Meghan had begun dating film producer Trevor Engelson.

in Los Angeles. Just seeing each other meant taking a five-hour plane ride. They eventually decided to divorce in 2013.

Filming *Suits* meant that Meghan had to be in Toronto for about eight months each year. Spending so much time in Canada was a big change for a young woman who had grown up in the California sunshine. But her friendships with the other cast members from the show made the time away from home fun.

Meghan and Trevor arrive at the Anti-Defamation League Entertainment Industry Awards Dinner in October 2011.

Meghan is seen here with her fellow Suits *cast members: Gina Torres, Rick Hoffman, Gabriel Macht, and Patrick Adams.*

She thought the fact that they all truly liked one another came through to viewers of the show.

Meghan could also relate to her own character of Rachel in many ways. She has shared that the show's creators did a great job of including certain parts of the

Meghan is also like Rachel in how much she values her education.

actors' personalities in their roles. Meghan, for example, describes herself as a foodie, a person who enjoys food and cooking. The writers gave Rachel this interest as well.

Meghan is also like Rachel in how much she values her education. In addition to the degree in communications Meghan has already earned, she has said that she

Meghan is seen here in the second season of Suits. *Meghan and Rachel Zane, her character on the legal drama, have a lot in common. For one thing, both women value education greatly.*

Meghan is seen here in the role of Rachel Zane during the fifth season of Suits.

would consider going back to school to earn a master's degree. She also deeply enjoys charity work. She has said, "[T]his type of work is what feeds my soul, and fuels my purpose."

From teaching young girls how to paint with watercolors to providing people in rural Rwanda with access to water, Meghan deeply enjoys spending her time helping others. For many years she worked with World Vision, even becoming the charity's global ambassador. Equality for girls and women is a cause mighty close to Meghan's heart.

5 BECOMING DUCHESS MEGHAN

During the summer of 2016, a friend set Meghan up on a blind date that would change her life. Before this time she knew little about Prince Harry—and vice versa. Growing up in the United States, Meghan wasn't terribly familiar with the royal family. And Harry had never watched *Suits*. The only thing Meghan asked her friend was whether the prince was kind. Their date went so well that they quickly followed up that first outing with two more dates.

Shortly after the couple's engagement, Harry told *People* magazine, "And then it was I think about three, maybe four weeks later

> **Growing up in the United States, Meghan wasn't terribly familiar with the royal family.**

Meghan and Prince Harry attend the wheelchair tennis event at the Invictus Games Toronto 2017 on September 25, 2017. The Games use the power of sport to inspire recovery, support rehabilitation, and generate a wider understanding and respect for the Armed Forces.

that I managed to persuade her to come and join me in Botswana. And we camped out with each other under the stars. She came and joined me for five days out there, which was absolutely fantastic." He shared that this time together was when they truly got a chance to get to know each other.

> **When they announced their engagement in November 2017, Meghan's life began to change intensely.**

Seeing each other wasn't always an easy task. Prince Harry's schedule was just as demanding as Meghan's, if not more so. When they realized how much they liked each other, they had to take advantage of every opportunity. Although this often meant traveling large distances, the new couple never went longer than two weeks without meeting up in one place or another.

When they announced their engagement in November 2017, Meghan's life began to change intensely. The following day, *Suits*

Prince Harry and Meghan announced their engagement to the world on November 27, 2017. They are seen here at the Sunken Gardens at Kensington Palace in London, England.

announced that Meghan would be leaving the show after its seventh season. She would now be dedicating her work life to the causes that Prince Harry champions through his work with the Royal Foundation.

Just days after they announced their engagement, Prince Harry and Meghan appeared together at the Terrence Higgins Trust World AIDS Day charity fair at Nottingham Contemporary. Meghan will now be dedicating her time to support Harry's Royal Foundation.

Through their Royal Foundation, Prince Harry and the Duke and Duchess of Cambridge teach others how to help members of their community. Their Coach Core apprenticeship trains young people with limited opportunities to become sports coaches and mentors in their communities. Prince Harry and Meghan are seen here taking part in a training class on March 8, 2018, in Birmingham, England.

On May 19, 2018, the couple wed in a highly celebrated ceremony at St. George's Chapel at Windsor Castle. Following the wedding, Meghan was given her new title—the Duchess of Sussex.

CHRONOLOGY

1981 Rachel Meghan Markle is born on August 4.

1987 Meghan's parents get divorced.

2003 She graduates from Northwestern University's School of Communication.

2011 Meghan lands the role of Rachel Zane on *Suits*. She marries longtime boyfriend Trevor Engelson.

2013 She and Engelson divorce.

2016 Meghan meets Prince Harry on a blind date.

2017 Meghan and Prince Harry announce their engagement. *Suits* announces that Meghan will not be returning to the legal drama.

2018 She weds Prince Harry on May 19.

FIND OUT MORE

Prince Harry. Official website of the British Royal Family.
https://www.royal.uk/prince-harry

The Royal Foundation of The Duke and Duchess
of Cambridge and Prince Harry.
http://www.royalfoundation.com/

WORKS CONSULTED

"5 Things to know about Prince Harry's fiancée, Meghan
Markle." ABC News, November 27, 2017. http://
abcnews.go.com/Entertainment/things-prince-
harrys-fiance-meghan-markle/story?id=46206775

Agard, Chancellor. "Meghan Markle is officially leaving
Suits after season 7." *Entertainment Weekly*, November
28, 2017. http://ew.com/tv/2017/11/28/meghan-
markle-leaving-suits/

Goulet, Matt. "Q&A: The Beautiful Meghan Markle on
Suits, Canada Day, and Handwriting." *Esquire*, July 17,
2013. http://www.esquire.com/entertainment/
interviews/a23925/meghan-markle-interview/

Mackelden, Amy. "Everything We Know About Meghan
Markle's Family." *Harper's Bazaar*, November 29, 2017.
http://www.harpersbazaar.com/celebrity/latest/
a13943391/meghan-markle-family/

Markle, Meghan. "Meghan Markle: I'm More Than An
'Other.'" *Elle*, December 22, 2016. http://www.elleuk.
com/life-and-culture/news/a26855/more-than-an-
other/

WORKS CONSULTED

Masters, James. "Prince Harry and Meghan Markle to wed on May 19, 2018." CNN, Updated December 15, 2017. http://www.cnn.com/2017/12/15/europe/prince-harry-meghan-markle-wedding-intl/index.html

"Meghan Markle." Biography.com. https://www.biography.com/people/meghan-markle-013117

Pearce, Tilly. "Meghan Markle—five quick facts about Prince Harry's fiancée after the couple got engaged." *The Sun*, December 3, 2017. https://www.thesun.co.uk/tvandshowbiz/3857535/meghan-markle-prince-harry-fiancee-facts/

Tauber, Michelle. "Why Meghan Markle Won't Be a Princess (But She'll Still Live in a Palace!)" *People*, November 27, 2017. http://people.com/royals/why-meghan-markle-wont-be-a-princess-but-shell-still-live-in-a-palace/

Wills, Ella. "Meghan Markle to give up charitable roles at the UN and World Vision Canada to start her royal life with a 'clean slate.'" *Evening Standard*, November 28, 2017. https://www.standard.co.uk/news/uk/meghan-markle-to-give-up-charitable-roles-at-the-un-and-world-vision-canada-to-start-her-royal-life-a3704426.html

GLOSSARY

calligraphy (kuh-LIG-ruh-fee)—a fancy form of handwriting

chameleon (kuh-MEE-lee-uhn)—a person who easily changes attitude or purpose

diverse (dih-VURS)—including more than one social, cultural, or economic group

humanitarian (hyoo-man-i-TAIR-ee-uhn)—one who is concerned with helping others

paralegal (par-uh-LEE-guhl)—an attorney's assistant

INDEX